Mallarmé descri
the poet doesn'
with deft and multiple shafts surrounds the place
where the core, the feeling, the meaning must be.
The truth of that likeness animates the intensity of
all poetry, especially poems that rely on imagery —
visual, of course, but tactile, auditory, olfactory too.
It is just here that Chernicoff's poems so dazzle
me, please me. She relies on the things of the
world, things we all share in the knowledge of, to
move her voice towards us. In her slow, slender
lines she invites collusion with the reader's breath,
so we find ourselves breathing along with the text,
startled by what she's just made us say. She leads
us into a sensuous world of vivid, unsentimental
love, love not just for bodies but for moves and
circumstances. They are our reward for breathing
with her.

—Robert Kelly, Series Editor

The Red Dress

Charms Troubled & Amorous

BILLIE CHERNICOFF

The Red Dress

Charms Troubled & Amorous

DR. CICERO BOOKS

www.drcicerobooks.com

Dr. Cicero Books
New York Rio de Janeiro Paris
First Edition
Manufactured in the United States of América
Distributed by Small Press Distribution, Berkeley, CA

ISBN: 069235414X
ISBN-13: 978-0692354148

Then lift up your voices, those organs of nature,
those charms to the troubled and amorous creature.

Ode to St. Cecilia, Henry Purcell, 1683

For Larry

CONTENTS

The Red Dress

Charms Troubled
& Amorous

Descending
to her own leitmotif.

Do you see her skip
out, red dress, aleph
fire escape, zed?

The heart twirls.
It zig zags.

She abandons her dress
and every apartment.

We are left with things to say.

Trade You

For that red dress
the tattered blue of forever.

For your destiny
a good laugh.

For the sublime, the naughty.

For a doctrine of doubts
a lexicon of light.

For your conspiracy theory
a girl to make you crazy.

Lazy, hazy, mazy.

For your promises
my let's see.

For that thunderbolt
a Cuban cigar.

For religion, alchemy.

For clarity, a secret.

For redemption, confusion.

For a mirror, a green lake
around our shoulders.

Oarsman

How muscle glides under skin
like his sleek boat through water.

He rows her, the woman, his wife?
Their little son? Across to somewhere
they can use the old words again
keen as blades.

Oarsman, I am the water.

For weeks he rows
through every book I read.
His back says so little.
Where are the words I wrote there
the explicit tarot?

He, the word, remains.
Would you challenge
the word oarer?

To no avail.
I do not part from him.
I, the water, part for him.

A word in the lips of others.
Oarsman, no less seductive.

I, the water,
become a book.

Nocturne

Night has hours
slow as haunches.

Night has a body
confusable with stone
and with bread.

Has a wolf
his howl not so
different from yours.

Has a hare
suave and busy
whose leap alarms
and round eyes gaze.

Night has a green plant
who thinks the moon
follows him like a bride
saying
      O wyrt,
my wort, my root,
my tobacco, oak moss,
coriander,
thy leaves are my people.

Ur

Brindle cow and cooking pot
husband's hand, wife's hip

whose religion says live near water
the laughter of women
syllables inscribed in clay.

Dust and cunning of the marketplace
saffron, musk, coins handed over.
The blind man with his wooden flute
the clamor of your childhood.

Deserere, the fragrance of water
your secret devotions.

It's a crime to look back though your life is on fire.

Longevity in love
is unnatural
like snake charming
and disappearing.

Even with elixirs to help men
understand the speech of women
with its floating, murmuring
cloud raising and cries.

It takes one to learn the names
one to read cracks in the sidewalk.
One to study ghosts, the other
to perfect the use of salt.
One to mend a sleeve.

One to breathe,
one to hear things
a thousand miles away.

Do you remember I jumped into the void
to test your hypothesis and we learned the difference?

Do you remember I waded into a vernal pool
and told you what it was like being a girl?

Do you remember I showed you a tarot card wasn't it
the hanged man, radiant yogi poet, peaceful Odin himself?

How I hid the ring you gave me in a stream to find it later?

Remember we observed a fish for forty days
and took notes?

Were happily afraid of snakes and the dark, wondering
at all the people who had become afraid of bread?

How your heart was a bull and my heart was a bull leaper?

Remember that we were loyal to Dante.

We still are.

About

Not about me the poem is
without reference to things
that did or didn't happen
in a dream in a paragraph
I read over a guy's shoulder
on the subway as we swayed
together under Paris
but that never happened
and the poem is not about him
is only occurring to me
and you, in time
a little musical calamity
like getting splashed
while you're whistling for a cab
rained on, hopeful
someone will pull over
so you can climb in
and close your eyes
listen or not
to the radio, listen
the poem is about you
if anyone, it's because music
makes words want to say something
a hum in the ear
a thrum you know where.

Dearest, a poem is only something
I read, a volume of influence
that makes me want to write back
because conversation

as the green snake said
is more quickening than light.

Don't think I wouldn't rather write about
the crisis, conflict, catastrophe
something other than the sky again.
But it's the sky that comes to me
in the morning like it's my responsibility.

An Education

I went to you
like kindergarten
where I discovered
my hand print
was my own and
I was a smart little thing
and squinting into
the sun made something
happen that might be
what people meant
by beautiful or might be
what people meant by
it's only your imagination.

You knew something
I wanted to know
so I went to you
like grammar school
where I studied
the slender discipline
of the sentence
the chant of
multiplication
as early music
as rapture
and prophecy
the athletic pleasure
of being fast
the pleasure of
a leathery thunk
in the mitt

and the strange feeling
I was sitting on something
flower-like I needed to
press against the bench.

I went to you
like high school
emerging from
the woods with
kitten heels
and gypsy etiquette
and the worst girl
in school seemed
to me the most
wonderful the most
free, and I learned
I wasn't the only one
who couldn't tell
my dreams from
what happens.

I went to you
like college where
I thought oh this
is what that's about
no wonder we're
all hiked up.

I'd be lost without you
comfortable neither sitting
nor standing.

You're the instructions
my mother left me
at the orphanage door
deciphered in secret
ecstatic rites after vespers.

I love you like milk & everything
that makes me uncomfortable later
the very things for which I lust.

It's no use closing the book
propped open like a basement window.

I am out of mothers
out of paper by the bed
and can't breathe unless
a field, without a window
open even in winter.

The sadness of mothers
overwhelms.

She who hoped that a cloth on the bed
a cloth with blue flowers would help.

What to do with two yards of damask
a husband who came home so late on foot
singing, his car somewhere
a daughter who slipped out even later.

Sometimes Anken's cattle escaped and grazed
our field bare all night.

How many words to make a church
that god will come down into
so you can meet her at last
in a glade of quiet breathing.

A church where you can ask her what to do
and her answer is the one who lives with you
who won't point a spade into earth
who waits for pebbles, weeds, generations of ants
to urge earth open with their little kindnesses.

You wait with her for the sacrament of rain
for the green presence of the plant
itself to rouse the light.

Without a word
she startles doves,
destroys comparisons.

If you're squeamish, don't prod the beach rubble.
Sappho

Shock of bare toes
in the beach yuck.
Glyphic rot, its own
small mist the salt air
never untangles.

Shaken by each
fragrant girl awake.

Wet green weeds
nacreous purple
lung-shaped shells
glisten and this fragile
transparent bladder with
violet tentacles stings.

Not the same purple of that cloth
shadowing one Cyprian cheek
that was yesterday.

The Desire of Language

We are each other's
golden hives & words
our hidden sighs.

Waking with this lingo
not in my head exactly
the words & I born together
into the day

      & the words feel
like my real body, made of
cool air, bird song
& crow talk,
an old cotton sheet.

Language longing
to walk with curious feet
into the day, we have one
collarbone, the same belly
& vulva, syllables of
the same night lingering
in the crook of our neck.

We two, each other's
pleasure & terror
so one must feel
with tenderest fingers
to know the difference.

Kore

Before the poem begins
there's something she sees
a strange light, say, only
the way it moves down the avenue
she wants to move with it.

That's not all, never all.

She imagines her own body
in language, lost.

Only a girl
descending
in her jouissance
erotic, mystical,
political like all poems
perverse, in that
she's already half in love.

A girl gone
a woman calling
down the dark wells
girls become
unwritten laws
ripen & flare
the mind taking fire
the threshing
blonde on blonde lyric
unanswerable she,
her couch in the barley.

Palimpsest

Albedo. At this stage
be not distracted
by peacock tail, or
other color or marvel
or promise of results.

Rather, note the trace of a rim
a fraction of incident light.

With your fingers, braille like
experience the tarnished still
luminous past.
Severus of Antioch
over Euclid's Elements.
Luke over Iliad.

More than one thing is true.

At a crime scene
objects over others unearth
a sequence & rhythm of
events, even motives
but there are lies
amnesia brought on by wine
the allure of complexity
slips of my tongue.

Recital

Schubert, unexpected
blondes in bustiers play him
songful, his lilting
defiance of syphilis,
his death near.

Are all poems love poems?

Shirts from countries
formerly of the Soviet Union
play Bartok.
It's ok to be restless
rummage for a pen
remember 12th grade
History, the teacher's
low drone, battles
in thick, too warm air
while I, girl narcissist,
imagined myself mostly
in the cars of bad boys,
the losers.

Beethoven, I breathe.
I no longer assume.

It's ok to be lonely,
scared of the dark.
What if my tether broke,
an outer space catastrophe
drifting through the vast
starry night past time, would
the silence be love itself?

Vulture, no one's
favorite color, unlike
hawk or eagle
those noble emblems
who help themselves
to the living.

Vulture, pacifist
economist, beatnik
monk eats humble.

Patron of coincidence
poet who waits alone
for what happens
for the tough or delicate
too wild to take home
meat we abandon
beyond desire
save his at last
his grand quiet wings.

The slowest most erotic
kiss of my life, waking
or dreaming, I'm falling
and you say I promise
never to do this with anyone
but you and I say please
do this with everyone.

I never married you that's the reason
we never divorced and still like
to make out the way one makes out
tiny print, holding it further and further
away till it says something like a boat
pushing off with us in it, all the way
to a little island that's ours.

Isn't that your ex-wife on the roof
playing the flute in her circus tulle and stars?
There's something she forgot to tell you
something she can tell you at last.
She lets down a ladder and knowing
it could be a trick you climb.
Her shoulders and bare feet still make you shy.
When she smiles you remember how to begin.
No need to say anything again.

Ever

since 300 A.D. in the geomantic city of Hangzhou where
we sifted language from the cloud that formed in the flask
of us,

when I remember the difference between the mid-day
clamor outside, and the room where divided by wooden
slats light fell over us in golden swathes in silence I wonder
if that was the substance we were looking for.

Or in Venice, in the shadows, sotto portico, barely out of
sight.

Some say Marco Polo invented Hangzhou and some that
he invented Venice, and rumors distill themselves over time
into lagoons and mirrors, poets and courtesans, our tercets
under the pines.

When I say the name of that perfume there are so many
letters my lips feel like they're kissing.

Have we not tried transmuting what makes us tremble into
treatises on devotional architecture or manifestos on its
staggering destruction at the hands of insects and infidels?

Our failures drown like handwriting in the green water of
the canal and we rush back to our hotel in the little piazza
of the white lion.

It was with you I lost my virginity, in the sense that I first
realized how hermaphroditic we are in love. You for
instance are a dark cave I long and fear to penetrate, leaving

my handprint inside you with ochre blown through a reed.

A flower going to seed in Burmese amber, one hundred million years old, and the wasp-like ancestress of bees are not lost on us.

Let nothing be lost on us. Bright shapes in air, the sense or scent of something tendered, as in the Tarot a hand emerges from cloud holding out a single pip. Not the symbol, but the actual instrument, the means.

We have been the naif sitting under a tree, oblivious, lost in romantic speculation. If he looks up, he will take the cup of pure feeling with no idea of the discipline it imposes. That is how it began with us, and that is how it begins.

Our conversation has long been the essence if not the whole of my spiritual practice, whether the speech of our bodies laboring toward ecstasy or the elliptical meanderings of breath through the larynx over the tongue and between the lips. In the midst of our conference opinions silence themselves as I become you.

Faux naive and faux wise by turns. I'm afraid there's no one else here.

Over time each pair of lovers writes its galateo, its book of courtesies and taboos, those things that make us laugh or swoon unfailingly and those we must never confess.

In Vienna I lay dreaming on the couch of Dr. X every afternoon at three for the three years of my analysis. Healing after all is a matter of rhythm, seductive fictions and the elixir of boredom. The analysand says the same

27

thing every day until it becomes meaningless, the analyst the same thing every day until it becomes meaningful. Then that too fails to soothe or perplex. The eye wanders in sunlight reading the motes, and we say that.

In one dream books fall from shelves and I shelve them differently, according to color of binding, ornamentation of font, date of publication, ciphers encoded in the marbled Italian endpapers, sheen of the gilded edge.

One might make of this a ballet, a pas de deux between a ballerina and her books. Books fall over and over, and she en pointe bends to lift them, to help them, finding places for them between others as if they were sad or shameful memories, until she herself falls into a deep prayerful crouch, and her diaphanous skirt settles around her in time, a sort of chrysalis woven of sunlight and things you've said to me.

What I had was the usual thing that can't be cured. Have. I conceal you in the past like an aria, an Orlandesque.

In Vienna, City of Dreams, we hold hands over a kaffee and kipferl and pay no attention to Marlene or the good Doctor himself under the brims of their fedoras. Our knees touch, golden crumbs fall into our laps, and we can't tell the past from the sweet future.

We dance at Schillerpark, close, so close, your lips at my ear. What do you want from me, really, you ask.

I imagine us fleeing like Schiller's robbers to the forest, fleeing like the poet himself to Leipzig and Jena.

"Live with your century but do not be its creature." Then it is possible to talk about the soul, about sacrifice and the sublime, to write everything, and to be together always.

If you want to know what I want from you, don't die.

We sneak through customs with innocent eyes and a suitcase full of language so old no one knows the truth.

There are shadows before there is light and snow drifts in the narrow streets, between the balustrades, in the manes of lions. Even the angels are vague, shrugging their small shoulders.

Everything that happens is something you mean or something to tell you. If I don't tell you now, I will tell you later.

At the End of the Day

to Robert Kelly

Sometimes something I write
tells me what really happened
or what the sky said
sometimes it's something you write
say or point to as you pointed out
the constellation of The Dragon
one winter night
the splendid arc of him
reaching across the sky over us
and the bright cloud of his speech
that would, you said, be visible
even if he hid himself.
Then a snowplow made a sound
that I dreaming heard as your great roar.

Cirque Tsigane

Arose
a red tent
our warmth
& waxy candles
fanned by an air
from nowhere.
Accordion.

A daughter
balances
on taut threads
of her mother's
praise.
Syllables
of her name
hidden
among others.

Slender cipher
an I in black
jongleur
does as he likes
with things
slips your heart
out of your chest
not only yours
but ever more
do what they
don't do
surprised by

their desires
& ours we sigh.

A horse & his ballerina
God's death & birth
canter by.

Under the Rose

1.

So nonchalant might dying be
slipping out of that shallow silk.

Love follows scent to its altars.
A rose in her very air.

Hold that color in mind
till thought gathers in the lungs
and lips shape the instant
as you are able
make visible all your animals.

2.

Who were we before language
before its disclosures
and persuasions,
the ordeals of becoming.

We cry out and guess why
all our likelihoods arise
from a logic itself conjured
by syntax, the magician.

3.

A staircase that goes only down.
This way to the shabby grimy
poorly lit palace
of things we never tell.

The exit must be close,
in the dark a voice saying
yes, me too.

4.

Our secrets are not ours
those things the gods
once hid in us, the roar
and the remedy, the sweet torah
the rabbis say, and fragrant

the clandestine pleasures hidden
by errata in the mind stream.

5.

Bardo of the rose.
Continual revelation
in the dark between
its tongue-like petals.

Between us.

We vortices, rays
petals, undulations
language made visible.

Would you say
we are very close?
Would you say we?

Ordinary Morning

1.

No invention to equal this light
this two note grace of the chickadee.

2.

Your scent on my fingers
beloved, warm as day.

3.

O muse of drunken girls
& careless love
mend my devotion to what is at hand.

4.

I'll sleep in his arms or another's.
You understand I think
the moon under your feet.

5.

Lire sans fin, Villon says
read without end.

6.

Ripe figs sway over us
tart green apples, chestnuts

thick on the ground
rose hips, long and slender.

A little snake I interview
black with yellow stripes
head lifted, awake
from the very beginning.

7.

Whose gifts are these
whose book held out for our pleasure?
As pleasure is something I can trust
though not as I trust the silence.

8.

Your name slipped into conversation
a hare in moonlight, music in the radio.

Agora

Looking at those giant
yet stumpy
sculptures of men
from the neck down
in Chicago, with
no heads, no arms
a whole flock of them
walking,
ugly men maybe
but from a distance
handsome crows
and crows are men
who can use tools
to open doors to more.
And they can talk.

Magdalena Abakanowicz
made these stalwart men
and I wonder how it was
to make people that asked
that much of her
that so few people
then liked.
Hardly anyone likes men.

She "wanted
to take a walk
among imaginary plants"
and men do sometimes
talk like trees.

I like the bark-like
texture of these civil men
who almost face each other,
thick and ridged like white pine.

You

You are the you of my poem
ever since we met in the clouds

or was it underground, that mouth
like cave in the earth, water
trickling down stone to a pool.

You're the one who takes me home.
The times I am most here
where I am, it's you.

Grandmother
wolf, woodsman
honeymoon
just born
curled on my belly
I call you
the name only I call you.

You bewilder me.
You're all verb.

In the night we tremble
in our alonenesses
my hand writing inside yours.

She, He

She made rain fall into a city.
He paved wet streets to her apartment.

She tried stars, lifting a text to their light.
He squeezed verbs into rapt substance.

She fashioned the heart of its fictions.
He rooted the day in green examining.

She welcomed him coming and going.
He knew her for his lost sister.

She dreamed of writing an inside out sentence.
He noticed the ocean colored dish wobble.

She reported the hellebore was up.
He reported all men were his rivals.

He found nettles by the river.
She brewed a tender cup.

He wanted to know something about her.
She could see nothing was like anything else.

He got the sudden lingo of birds.
She the fish, the shell, the hush.

She brought him the first radish.
He brought her something on a ship.

She had an alchemic urban poise.
He was drawn to weird lights in Vermont.

Winter she said was a myth of her country.
Her body he said was a myth of his.

She poured water.
He hollowed a reed.

She mistook doves for owls.
He heard cars on the road.

She made the lake cohere.
He woke at the border of her.

He was late to the wedding.
She sneaked in all mussed.

She walked around among him.
He invented science to answer her

but that wasn't the answer.

Alchemilla Vulgaris

The boyish lesbian philosopher at the bridal shower
who seemed even more than the bride to be our center
and who was so relaxed in her clothes, in her body
long married, passed along what a long married
neighbor of hers upstate had once said to her
about marriage, and it had proved over time to be true.

Sometimes it's dry.

The way she said it was wry and rueful, just a little
flirtatious, so you could tell how much she loved her wife
and how much fun they had together.

Then a few days later, after a playful evening
you dreamed I climbed the stairs
to bring you two glasses of water, one in each hand.

In the right hand, a flute of clear water
tinctured with Elm, rhymes with whelm
for when you're drowning,
in the left, my writing hand, a glass of drops
gathered from the edges of leaves, Lady's Mantle
sounding so mystically and euphemistically sexy, and it is
with its velvety ruffled leaves, the way they catch the dew.

Clues

Something
cheekier.

Love refracted
dear things of the dead.

Leap inhabit my whim
lacquered up.

Tongue marauder
ear keeping vigil.

Unstruck bell,
little boat of knowing.

No head, no headache
disheveled assurances.

Two under linden
& little bird.

Black pearl or
market, stockings.

Spangled context
for maiden, hound.

Intimacy of river
swimmer evident.

Loamy word
crossed out.

Conjugal love
cymbals.

Difficult honey,
daily salt or laud.

Oh Wood
Anemone.

Mere nearness
derails.

Practices

Turn wine to water listen ear cupped
gentle story husband glad face home
from market fresh fish too.

Marvel light held in octagon
lie on floor look up into
dome, decipher.

Sweep house clean not too
clean, crumbs for mouse
books for sorrow.

Lift stone on stone, balance
fragile veins all doing undone
edge between tilled and wild.

Heart's motives unfold
shadows half light
half thievery.

This language rafts abstract
I back to not I, not me, push
hard for muddy bank.

Luminous slip under tent
soft air I meant
no underpass, jazz.

Let creamy Porsche cup
of warm eve top down
back of town hall.

Ritually undress armor to wings to most
ephemeral undies a rhythmic tease conceals
and reveals not without irony that would be music.

The Hours

Heart up a tree roots in water
angels in their zones deliver
sticks in bundle, house in glade
a way to be content for an hour.

Falling over a dark verge
a web holds fast.
Orion, low on horizon.
Go back to bed go back
under the sea & make salt.

A godly breeze
touches you & summer
makes you wise as herbs.
Finding & bending to each
in its hour.

Cool cellars of Detroit
jars of cherries ruby red.
Creak of porch swing, hum
of conversation, slipping away
to wilding orchard, warm grass.
Beauty undid me once & for all.

How we loved each other
as in a dream the sea gave salt
the mild air shone on our sins.

Let me make amends among
trees, their cool speaking.
I'll find your spine, bones of
legs arms fingers cock, staves
of an honest man leafing up.

I'm a fool, a green branch
bareheaded in weather
I'll never wise up, so slay me
with the only craft that matters.

Broke cars & lost men
move past how quiet
we make our eyes.
We steal ourselves
under the moon plums
from somewhere then.

A sprig of velvet wort an offering
in my church of senses, wand
or words I follow an earful of
spirits, ancestors of the steppes.

Every hour leaves me
that is you leave me
a gypsy cloud or handful
of Pearly Everlasting
tied to a fence with string.

At twilight my frail carriage
admits the dark at a gallop.
Then an owl knows best.

I dive in over my head for you
play by the sea harper,
take me with you.
Lured fishermen drown so.

The sea comes in at last
nothing I count on is weird.
I'll steer by this new moon
tea leaves, salt rime.

Give me your newfangled.
I know what to do with
signs, ruins, desire.
Lust. Shush now.

I'm a fool again
a vernal loser
I lose myself.
Surprised by death,
rise someone else.

Is this music I can't tell
any from else.
In the morning how to begin?
No stars, no horse, no bird on the sill.

56

Gone, all but stark particulars.
Find again in emptiness
a web of lights strung above.
When I'm looking,
I'm looking for the truth.

What can be said that's true of this
or any day outside the wine-like
mineral scent of noon.

Thanks for the peaches
& what you meant by them
this time of year when it's hard
remembering. Modest signs
of forgiveness thus.

Much ripens hidden
under the moon we eat
some give some away
more alive than before.

Moonlight over roof milk.
Two trees, a little snake
& other lessons.

Nothing's perfect but we're home now.
Oil the rusty handle, pump cold water up.

My new moon
my Ouija board
my here I am
my never mind
my love you still.

I know where morels throng
a downed oak too & other
prosy things where the river is.

Vrais Semblants
Six to Sarah Moon's Photographs

1. Une Femme Sans Titre

Peeking through the lotus
of her hands
without a name
in the articulate lotus
of her clothes, silk
fitted to her exact
thighs hips pelvis waist
that waterline
where sepals dip back
into their images.

2. Bluecrest

Decipher this garment
this jeweled cage
where imprisoned she
awaits her enchanted suitor.
He in the body of a bird
comes and goes seven years.
She studies Latin
procrastinating, but in love
with a bird prince must
at last have him as he is.

Their children have wings.
Every love story ends here.

3. A Below the Waist Love Story

Lying on her back in sunlight
feet close to the edge of the lake
leather shoes with lace stockings
her long dark wool skirt fallen so
peacefully between her legs
everything above her waist outside the frame.
The sedge is infinitely delicate.
There are water lily leaves, but no blossoms.

Try to remember what happened here.

4. Dimanche

A woman walking away
turns back to look.

She could be the one lying by the lake earlier
you about to make love to or strangle her
or having made love you saunter behind
made glad by her hips in her skirt, wondering
whose bike this is and whose little dog.

5. And Now My Lovely Assistant Will

give you the illusion of water
flowing back into her past.
Body arched back, arms flung
back, throat and armpits exposed
as if to a knife thrower
open fingers surrendered
the reticulate beauty of
her pulse under her ribcage
dark plume of hair splayed
over the water turning to wing
her fine head a bird's.

6. Coïncidences

How many women down how many roads
how many bare breasts through tulle reiterate
red lips, red chipped nails, petals who could count
these women with wings with pale globes
with bones with couture with tiny stitches
one after another with signatures with sequins
how many emblems of desire how many lost gloves
how many horizons are shoulders whose hoofs are hers
how much intentional corrosion how much accidental sky
over the ox-bow through grass winding dreamlike
why this man and not another
so many women with hands over faces
like leaves like flecks in their eyes like chandeliers
naked women in ateliers like chairs like pears bound
in paper with string in a row with reflections
who is the witness of all this seeming?

So many paths leading into the sky,
rooks wheeling over.

Since You Asked

The truth is a moth clinging to the screen
the sky against us all day.

The truth is the first bird I tell you.

The truth is, when a sentence begins who knows?

The truth is its work forgetting, no apostrophe.

The truth looks up at you all naughty.

The truth stands you up for lunch.

The truth sways, strays and hunkers down.

The truth untangles a thread
heaves a stone from a furrow.

The truth is hushed in fur in Russia.

The truth unbuttons all the little buttons of her gloves.

The truth is in a book as soon
as you take it in your hands.

The truth pares it down and uproots the smallest strand.

The truth is a huge luminous winged victory.

The truth is a mythic country without geographical
or anatomical verity, like the waist.

The truth is originally Arabic.

The truth is always afterwards.
Commentary and marginalia.

The truth balances on the rim of a fountain.

The truth is my cluttered apartment.

The truth is it doesn't matter that much.

The truth is as sad as an aquarium.

The truth is we have all this while
others only their gentle brown eyes.

The truth is fierce and unnatural
like so many blades of grass.

The truth wears a skirt a size too small.

The truth is only clouds telling you.

The truth imprints itself on water
and you can drink it.

The truth is elsewhere. A soldier
in a hot country, cello in a far room.

The truth is as delicate as lust.

The truth is as lusty as two of a kind.

The truth smells like bread.

70

The truth pushes aside the last rime of winter.

The truth is a damp green glyph in a teacup.

The truth is a furtive kiss in a hallway.

The truth is, Paul Celan said, a rumbling
walking among men amidst the metaphor squall.

The truth looks into the mirror for hours
tries on everything in the closet.

The truth plunders your conclusions
gives away everything you own.

The truth makes things difficult
but less necessary.

The truth is life can't explain itself any better
than a man holding your glance longer
than he should.

The truth pockets things for which it has no use.

The truth leaves the phone off the hook.

The truth is it won't be long now.

The truth is all wars are civil wars.

The truth is what Keats said.

The truth is more specific.

The truth is we happen to each other
where else is there to go?

The truth is the book I fell asleep reading
the sheet frayed a little at the edge
like a voice saying darling, oh darling.

Alba

1.

I floated in the eye of a gull
combed a sentence in a mirror
scattered some seeds in the air
the air took them into its mouths.
There is nothing to say but blue flowers
a hundred tiny blossoms on a stem.

Mosaic, multiply what was alive
by something even more alive
a Francis of fragments
water for Pliny's doves I look up
to see if any birds comment
but I'm not fast enough.

2.

Tears, most difficult salt only
the world knows how a day
breaks in countless mirrors
near is far & you're lost in mist
when love stands up in you again
& that is how a tale begins.

3.

A dream in love
with everyone
the moon so
round & smug
its fringe of lace
pure theater.

Sorry, moon.
Pearl in the folds
of that silk
kimono the sky,
palace of the divine
void, never empty.

Hole full of milk,
may I never speak
your faults again
nor anyone's, nor say
the thing I think, let me
say something else.

4.

Else I fail to wake you.
I am a prince if I am the one
& all who serve you stir.
To arms, daughters!
Fiery words to wound or bless
a day, if need be, a man.

5.

Dreams fill in the gaps & we
decide less than we think,
never in poems if we're true.
The one I wanted to write
this morning was Duncan's
Torso, the way a woman would.

"And the poem knelt in the rosy light of the ake."

6.

Magenta, genital rose
distilled twilight crowned
queen of the alphabet, Magdalene
whose consort is the green
of an olive grove Christ a leafy teacher
one ever found with the other.

More explicit than numbers is desire
the desire of light that creates the eye,
light that had been invisible, mystical to us
will soon lift & break our hearts with color
we lovers of the Ur-moon, beholder & beheld.
Nothing the other side of the mirror.

Silence

*"For one came headlong in the morning, dismembering me with a
sword and tearing me asunder according to the rigor of harmony."*
Visions of Zosimos

Is there a sound all music strives to come to in time
itself an instrument most resembling a door?

Does the arcane structure of the ear
helix conch canal pyramid anvil porch
bear the anatomy of the sound
so we can't hear it there, related
by a messenger so ardent and accurate
he himself becomes the message,
speaks directly to the heart.

Tongue of flesh, tongue of fire, in the exercise
of this twin address I have developed such
an acute stutter it hardly makes sense to tell
anything but the truth, or those lies only
sacred to love, themselves perhaps
the chaste water they won't hold.

The most lonesome of our devotions
is the practice of an alert, hunter-like stillness
between not always overtly musical events

resembling nothing so much as falling
in which the constant accompanying fear
of that swift, naked descent serves
as a slim-hipped, light-eyed guide
into the very aforementioned heart of it.

Crucible of a breath and a dewy chemistry
a day is what music we make of it.

I think it's love comes in the morning
with bright sword to nail or unmake us
according to the rigor of harmony.
The undoing of syntax and memory,
all our soft crimes, till we have nothing
are nothing.

Silence.

We can only come close.

Imparadis't

Imparadis't in one another's arms.
—John Milton, Paradise Lost

Folio of all your faces I wed
the last hours of day, hours of salt
come without any sadness at all.

You elicit dew from air you elicit yes
light falls all over itself for you that
kind of love can't help it.

Each letter of the alphabet another child
we conceive amidst scattered books
forts and apple trees full of ours.

Falling what a fresh thing to do
asleep in grass a body breathing I
remember the future better than the past.

Your night so often my morning fills
one the cup of the other after a time, time
is only an animal in the woods you hear.

Whatever you lost is still somewhere
molecules of an afternoon exhaled
from some other lips far away.

An ode in the morning from an Odalisque
gold for her goldfish and gold for her finch
a harem of dreams in her gaze reveals.

Secret revels of a happy woman
who never loves a thing for the last time
a little bird perched on her finger.

What a thing is a man, the ears of a satyr
with bulging eyes and a lewd tongue
a forehead furrowed with love.

He had an ironic bone in his body
a growl in its voice even a glance
vexed to friendliness.

In the half light of love a quiet
no consequence thronged dark wood
disturbs nor palace of light persuades.

What we intend the wind knows better
your ear whispers to my lips, unfurls
a single day the likes of never.

Clamor of crows what now is that your father?
Your mother sunlight on your closed eyes?
Clatter of bangles falling to the floor?

The blue the fugitive hour upon us
a bridge if you read me flows over a river
language made before we were born.

Linger ghazal of mute tension the singular
thorn of illicit love and charm of longing
a veined lyric wet flanks in pursuit.

A good slap to get your attention
give me my horse give me my mantra
I'll tell anyone who's on the way.

A charm like a mirror and one like a pitcher
be careful the spell that has to be broken
every daughter her silver word.

Enough year, take this hour this minute
take off your shoes and describe this brook
now forget every poem you know by heart.

All the words before "but" dissemble.
Who was sobbing before, who after?
What have you come to with your hands?

Be the good doctor
who translates a malady
saying something to make a man brave.

No glade love, let's to Van Eyck's
Chancellor Rollin's virgin city go
walk the streets close, hold hands.

Dwell on thy mystic couch evoke
moon evoke months evoke moths
evoke the quiet antidote to fear.

Every reason is a lie believe me
a mood is a girl bored with waiting
dark hair round her finger furled.

Only an apple's more ancient than
blame dear, the rough bark
sweet juice in your lips.

A crossroads, a cross, a crisis, a quest
to be born in the house that can heal you.
How the air around X trembles.

Blame the sky for being you
honey, bellow like that and bees
fly up sting you all confused.

O what is sweeter than anxiety
more quaint than lust, more
personal than little bees?

Shoo fly somber dreamy emblems
don't bother my nocturne my pretty nature
I feel I feel I feel so very Venusian.

I depend on the renaissance of flesh
documentary of a vague religion
if you don't mind mine.

Shadow of cloud or document
of ascent our failures redeemed
borne with each breath up.

A body's a crisis in the sky
a fuselage with its own intentions
bright with morning sleek with you.

Flights deferred and clothes defeated.
Tender lure of bread and morning
first naked foot on the floor.

Encouraged by apples informed
by clouds a day to pluck
from the sky again.

Acquiescence elusive amoral
fruit plucked from silence whatever
you thought not to say said yes.

Yes to grace and yes to gladness
yes to a stutter, it's so like bebop!
Yes to a mattress on the floor.

Let me be your lunar colander
sift the broth of you through me
o moon, trembling for Lorca.

A tremble dance in leafy vernacular
now your pale nape and every particular
gather, the moon one night to full.

Aye for alder, be for birch, ache
or glade your temple I tryst you
where your language comes from.

Wind belayed fire, ardent rogue
healing of the wood, doe leaping
from that bright ache in her chest.

A thorn from paw plucked
each plucker her glad quest
each quest its healed beast.

All my feelings are in the dictionary
this forest, fuck, and all the f words
then glad and glade us in the gloaming.

How did we come here, whose
handsome hands lifted us over
whose daughters were we once?

White horse of ancestral dreaming
windfall apples and wood for the taking
your father whistling after silence.

Caught her a silver fish in the morning
when they were young and slender
and fed on the gleam of things.

Who can bear to be apart from
the sky, its delicate steeples
the people written in our hands.

How did we not fall then fall?
The earth lifted herself up and we
lowered ourselves with a sigh.

No more motive than morning
braiding and braiding gold
strands in the sky.

Despite wings she dreamed
she wrote with bare feet
und der Schnee lügt nicht.

And the snow didn't lie, detours
in her spelling translatable
if you stayed close.

Word for word like Hölderlin's Pindar
then she lifted those wings
and you were lost.

To read one thing by writing another
a field of snow to improve my vocabulary
lost was what I was looking for.

I wake up words in my voice
and don't know what you mean
by the sky again only darker.

Under a crow moon
in a dark wood
no lostness in us.

A couch of leaves our dreams bring
sleep and news and meat we love
to our sorrow and delight.

A dreamer's always wrong about her dreams
talk so much smoke a body proposes
ever more sacred misunderstandings.

Say the word a word undoes
roses from air not artifacts these
rituals for our table with four legs.

Or cup, mirror, glove, horse
a world made out of the world only
changed. With both hands.

A cup of her own making.
With both hands so holy That descends
into wine, even into the painting of it.

Where shall I send thee the magician's
question, my own strength my dove
go everywhere, return to me.

Return to me my love the ordinary
our 'thousand decencies'
this paradise.

Of bees, still
no hard freeze
their hum

both high and low, and crabapples
hundreds this year, tiny golden globes
that bend the branches down.

The bitterness of walnuts
beauty of a friend's wife
was winter, quietly winter
always was. Then
a fen, or weir was it
March, a dream holding
water holding a fish
a word shaped voice
or voices, the waters of
a mystery that won't ache
the mind like April will
the twigs, the small
familiar plurals
heartbreaking
adverbs of cause
or place, nature verbs
worship verbs, rare
nonsense, useful promising
names of names swept away
by morning it's May almost
a lake in your lap.

Acknowledgments

I would like to thank Carey Harrison, John Keller and Robert Kelly, the good doctors at Dr. Cicero Books.

To Robert Kelly, whose work goes ever before, my gratitude for his keen reading of this text and his thoughtful suggestions.

My grateful thanks to those who read these poems early on, especially to Larry Chernicoff, who read them first over my shoulder.

And a thank you to Inpatient Press, who published the poem Ur, online.

Billie Chernicoff was conceived in the Free Hanseatic City of Hamburg by a soldier and a ballerina, born left handed in Detroit, and educated at Bard College. She raised a daughter in the Berkshire hills of Massachusetts where she lives with her husband and writes. She has worked as a printer, editor, teacher and gardener. Her book, *The Pleasures*, was published online in 2014 by Metambesen, at http://www.metambesen.org/books/. A book called *A Drop* is forthcoming in 2015 from Lines Chapbooks.

To the memory of my beloved mentor, the distinguished Brazilian educator, Dr. Emanuel Cicero, born in 1907 in Ubatuba, São Paulo. Rector of the College of Rio Grande do Sul from 1943 to 1978, he died in 1988 in Lisbon.

—Maximiliano Reyes, publisher

-FIM-

DR. CICERO BOOKS

19571016R00073

Made in the USA
Middletown, DE
26 April 2015